I0201086

The Curious Occurrence of Life

Also by Dimitri Chakhov

The Little-known Jesus' Teaching: *Evolve Your Mind*

The Curious Occurrence of Life

*How Genetic Code
Proves God*

Dimitri Chakhov

DC books

Previously published as *Digging under the Tree of Life*
Text copyright © 2020 Dimitri Chakhov
All rights reserved
ISBN: 978-1-989696-15-6

All Scripture quotations are taken from
THE HOLY BIBLE, NEW INTERNATIONAL
VERSION®, NIV® Copyright © 1973, 1978, 1984,
2011 by Biblica, Inc.™ Used by permission. All rights
reserved worldwide

The Cover image ID 140341678 © Mikhail Makeev
| Dreamstime.com

"The Spirit gives life."

(John 6:63 NIV)

Table of Contents

1. The Bet

My Friend Ben

"Do you believe in God?" I asked my best friend Ben.

It was a hot Friday afternoon in late summer. We were sitting in his backyard drinking beer. Ben looked at me with suspicion.

"I mean, not in the fanatical way, but as a smart, curious individual?" I asked. "What do you think? Is there somebody above us?"

"I don't see anyone," Ben said as he looked at the blue cloudless sky. "Do you see anybody?"

"Don't be stupid," I said. "Don't you know that reality goes a little bit deeper than your vision?"

"You get what you see," he said. "Don't hope that there is more."

"But how do you know?" I said.

"Scientists are smart dudes," he said. "They've searched everywhere and they haven't found God."

"What about our intellect?" I said. "How did it come to be?"

"Evolution," he said, wagging his pointed finger in my direction.

"Do you believe in evolution?" I said.

"You don't have to *believe* in evolution," he said softly smiling. "It's a scientific fact."

"It's not a fact, but a theory," I said.

"Scientific theory is the same thing as a fact," he said.

"Let's drop all the science talk," I said. "What do you personally think, as an individual? Does God exist?"

"I don't think about that," he said.

"Why?"

"Man, what's wrong with you today? All these questions. I don't have time for this kind of stuff. I'm a busy man."

"Alright, alright, so, do you think the Lions will beat the Bears on Sunday?" I said.

That day, I learned that spiritual conversations don't go well on Friday afternoons. You shouldn't ambush people with your deep inquiries when they are trying to relax and drink cold beer.

Does God Truly Exist?

Don't get me wrong, Ben isn't an oblivious person. He just has no interest in spiritual questions. He knows a lot about electronics and mechanics, and I admire his persistence. He always gets what he wants.

He would make a much better religious believer than me if spiritual ideas were ever to settle in his mind. He would pursue his ideas no matter what. For me, on the other hand, temptations often ruin my good intentions.

For example, I wanted to quit drinking because I thought that alcohol doesn't suit a spiritual soul. Yet, it's so tempting to have a beer with friends on a hot lazy Friday afternoon after a long workweek. I fail to make this small adjustment one week after the next.

I also have the tendency for doubts.

Does God truly exist? How would I know for certain that He does? These types of questions regularly pop into my head.

Oh yeah, I forgot to mention. That year, I discovered the Gospel. Reading the teachings of Jesus was an amazing intellectual and spiritual journey for me. My worldview began to change. But even so, I had trouble adjusting my life to match my changing views.

The Spirit

Sometimes, I felt like I was insane. Isn't it obvious that the world is a soulless place, governed by merciless laws of nature? Everyone who is born is bound to die. What am I trying to find? Why can't I accept reality as it is? Why do I get so lost in doubts and questions instead of enjoying my life?

I had all these doubts, yet some stubborn part of my mind didn't want to settle for the obvious.

That evening, I opened the Gospel. I found this verse and read,

> *"The Spirit gives life; the flesh counts for nothing."*
> *(John 6:63)*

The Greek word πνεῦμα (pneuma) is translated as the spirit, and it has a few meanings:
- a movement of air
- the breath of a living being
- the vital principle by which the body is animated
- the rational power by which humans feel and think[i]

"According to Jesus, the spirit is the key element of reality," I thought.

The problem was that when I read the Gospel, I believed Jesus. I believed in God. But in all the other times, I doubted my beliefs. For example, the rational power of the mind seemed to me to be dependent on the brain.

"As far as we can observe," I thought, "no intellect can exist without a brain. Isn't this evidence that the intellect is secondary to the body?"

Indeed, your observations give little support to Jesus' claim. Wherever you look, in the farthest corners of the universe or in the smallest particles of matter, you can't see the Spirit. Was my friend Ben correct? The sky is empty, and there is no God.

Was I fooling myself with a fantasy?

Is it insane to believe in God?

Is it insane *not* to believe in God?

I jumped back and forth in my thoughts, unable to make up my mind.

Let's take Ben as an example. He has a strong, well-rounded personality. I'm a weak and jealous soul. Why do I feel the need for God and he doesn't? Is it because he fits well in life and I don't? Do I subconsciously feel that I need help? Do I feel that only God can help me? Why am I so desperate?

The Theory of Evolution

The scientific theory of evolution by natural selection is often used to explain life's origins. The theory consists of two main ideas.

The first is that the development of life happens as a chronological series of changes that move from simple to complex. The second is that the driving forces of life's evolution are random changes aided by the process of natural selection.

The intent of the theory is rational. It attempts to explain the origins of life with simple concepts and excludes an elusive invisible Spirit (God-Creator) from these explanations.

At some point, I realized that the theory of evolution was standing in my way. It was the source and cause of my doubts. If we can explain everything without God then more likely, there is no God.

Yet, I felt that there was something wrong with the theory. What was it?

"I must understand the problem on my own terms," I thought.

Suddenly, I felt the excitement in my heart. It was at 10 p.m.

I grabbed my phone and texted Ben. "I'll disprove evolution."

"Let me know when you quit," he replied. "I'll buy you a beer."

The next minute, I thought, "Am I crazy? How am I going to disprove a scientific theory if I don't have any scientific qualifications?"

The stubborn element of my mind was telling me not to quit just yet. Details are always complex and often confusing, and it's hard to see the whole picture if you pay too much attention to them. I knew I had to look at the whole picture.

2. The Flowers Argument

The Grass in the Field

"Is there anything strange in the world, something that doesn't fit the theory of evolution?" I thought the next evening.

I looked out the window. The world was a familiar and routine place. I couldn't observe any anomalies.

After struggling with it for a few days, I decided to look up in the Gospel. Does Jesus use any arguments in support of his vision? I found a few passages and, at first, they didn't impress me at all. Below is one of Jesus' arguments:

> "And why do you worry about clothes? See how the flowers of the field grow. They do not labor or spin. Yet I tell you that not even Solomon in all his splendor was dressed like one of these. If that is how God clothes the grass of the field, which is here today and tomorrow is thrown into the fire, will he not much more clothe you - you of little faith?" (Matthew 6:28-30)

Jesus invites you to look at elements of your surroundings, to *"see how the flowers of the field grow."* Certainly, the natural settings you find yourself in are magical and beautiful. Yet, it's hard to agree with Jesus' claim that if God clothes the grass, He will also clothe the faithful.

Jesus misses an important logical connection. His conclusion that God will clothe the faithful is based on the premise that God clothes the grass. Yet, we don't know that God clothes grass; this statement needs to be proven by itself.

The flowers argument doesn't stand a chance from a practical point of view either. We produce clothes by means of labor and, literally speaking, faith alone can't dress anyone. It seems that Jesus fails to develop any logical support to his ideas and appeals instead to a blind trust.

Then I read the verses again and thought, "Wait a minute. Jesus compares the beauty of a field full of flowers to the design of clothing. Designers achieve results by using their vision, hands, pens, paper, computer software, and, ultimately, their intellect. Flowers don't have tools at their disposal, and yet their elegance easily competes with styles from the best fashion designers."

So how do flowers get their beauty?

Things get even more interesting if you look at plants from a purpose point of view. Plants' roots have a purpose to anchor and support the plant and to absorb water as well as minerals from the soil. The purpose of the leaves is to convert the energy from sunlight to produce sugar. The purpose of flowers, seeds, and fruits is reproduction.

The purposeful character of plant parts is puzzling. According to the theory of evolution, a plant evolved and developed through a long chain of random changes spanning across many generations. But how were random changes able to build the functioning and purposeful components of plants?

The Flowers Argument

Religious and spiritual beliefs are frequently associated with blind faith. Many leaders and preachers of the Christian religion contributed to such a perception. Martin Luther said, "Reason is the greatest enemy that faith has; it never comes to the aid of spiritual things."[ii]

However, this view is quite misleading. Jesus expects you to think rationally when he asks you to compare the beauty of the flowers to the design of clothes. To produce a beautiful dress, a tailor uses his natural talents and learned skills.

"Jesus' point is that the beauty of living things can't happen by blind chance either," I thought.

How solid is Jesus' argument? Clearly, it contradicts the theory of evolution.

But the logic behind Jesus' observation doesn't differ from the logic of physics. For example, you have never seen or touched gravity, but you know it exists. You can observe the effects; the gravitational force on Earth gives weight to physical objects. Gravity gives objects a physical property (weight), which is why gravity is called a physical force.

Jesus invites you to observe the elements of life. The existence of life tells you that there must be some force, perhaps also unseen, that's responsible for life's development.

The components of life are clearly purposeful. What does this fact tell you about the quality of the force that created them? This force needs to comprehend what purpose is, right?

You believe in gravity not because you can see it, but because you can observe its effects. Jesus' argument is similar. You observe beautifully designed living things. Some components of life, like a human mind, even carry intellectual capacity.

According to Jesus, you should expect the existence of an invisible force capable of producing such astonishing effects.

3. The Mixed-Up World

Science vs. Religion

While doing my research, I found a few amusing facts about science and religion.

It is often perceived that science and religion are incompatible and opposing branches of human thought. Surprisingly, religious and scientific viewpoints on the origins of things aren't so different. Both religion and science agree that at some point in time, there was no universe, and then the universe was created. The difference is in the details. Science insists that the big bang caused the universe, while religion is certain that the universe was created by God-Creator.

According to the religious view, God is the supreme authority over everything. Science insists that the powers that keep the universe in order are physical laws. Science assigns the physical laws the same attributes that religion assigns to God: true, universal, omnipotent, absolute.[iii]

Practically, both worldviews agree with a necessity for an omnipotent, absolute power. Unified reality is possible because of some universal authority.

Science allocates authority to the physical laws, while religion praises God as the supreme authority.

Religion and science agree that there was a time when life on Earth didn't exist. Again, the difference is in the details. According to science, life evolved thanks to random changes and natural selection. According to religion, life was created by God-Creator.

The Mix-Up

Science puts forward more explanatory concepts (the Big Bang, physical laws, and evolution, just to name a few) than religion, which has one answer for all questions—God-Creator. At this point, you might feel that science is intellectually the more attractive option, since it gives you the freedom to explore the universe.

However, scientific freedom is limited to physical causes. The physical causes have different names, but it is always the same idea: all events should be explained by physical forces and physical matter.

You may notice the mismatch. Science embraces knowledge and reason but denies the existence of the mind and soul. This leaves you with the question: Where do knowledge and reason supposed to come from?

Religion claims that the intellectual force of God lies in the origin of all things. The human mind resembles the qualities of the Supreme Being. You might suppose that religion should embrace thinking as the most significant quality of a human soul.

But in practice, religion often promotes blind faith and unquestioned obedience among its followers. Such an attitude suppresses free thinking and intellectual development.

Two Types of Inquiry

Let's compare the religious and scientific methods of inquiry.

Any scientific inquiry seeks new knowledge about the surrounding world. New knowledge must come in the form of testable explanations. The scientific method includes the following steps: formulating a question, making observations, forming a hypothesis, conducting an experiment, and drawing conclusions.

The key element of a scientific hypothesis or theory is it must be supported by observations or experiments.

But what are the steps of religious inquiry?

I searched the Internet and I couldn't find any.

"Does religious inquiry into reality consist of only one step?" I thought. "This step would be blind and unbending trust in every word of the Bible."

At this point of my own journey, I felt a strong disappointment with religion. My goal was to find understanding. I knew for sure that I would never accept blind faith.

Often, secular propagandists paint religious beliefs as illogical and irrational opinions, and at that moment, I began to think the same. You can observe neither God nor the heavenly kingdom, so believing in such things must be naïve.

I spent the next few days mired in doubts.

"Is my inquiry over?" I thought with sadness.

Poor Quality Input

Then I decided to play smart and use some scientific methodology to get me out of this funk.

First, I needed to formulate a question. It was easy. Darwin's theory claims that random changes have the capacity to produce meaningful and functional results. Is it a plausible idea?

Next, I needed some observations that either supported or rejected Darwin's claim.

At that time, I often worked from home. In the evening, after I had turned off my computer, my lovely three-year-old daughter would sit in my chair and hit the keyboard. One day, I realized that it was a much-needed observation.

Let's imagine that, in imitating her parents, a toddler randomly types on a keyboard day after day. The computer automatically saves her typing. Would these files have any meaning?

This example is not so far off from reality. Changes to living beings are achieved by modifications in DNA, which can be likened to a code. Imagine that a toddler types into the source code file of a smartphone app. The file was left open by her father, a software developer. An excitedly typing toddler is a relatively accurate representation of random changes.

Would she be able to improve the source code? Would she be able to add a new feature to the program while randomly hitting the keyboard?

As they say in the IT world, garbage in, garbage out.[iv] The saying is used to express the idea that incorrect or poor-quality input will always produce faulty output. The theory of evolution suggests something entirely different. According to the theory, a random input into genetic code has produced functional and beautiful living beings.

"What do you say about this, Ben?" I thought as I imagined our discussion. "Don't you see the issue here?"

4. The Greatest Mystery of All

DNA and Information

Who is right: Jesus or Darwin? Maybe, the universe is a messy, illogical place, crazy things happen, and meaningless input leads to meaningful results.

It's also possible that the universe is a rational, logical place and—crazy thing—God exists!

It's possible that reality is stranger and deeper than you can ever imagine! Yet, I decided to hold the wild horses of my imagination and stick to the facts.

For the next few weeks, I tried to learn a little bit about genetic code. In the end, I firmly understood one thing: DNA and RNA molecules carry genetic information.

The English word "information" was derived from the Latin verb *informare* (to inform) in the sense "give form to the mind, teach, instruct."[v]

Today, the word has two common meanings: as data (in information technologies), and, in other situations, as "knowledge acquired through experience or study."[vi]

Message, information, meaning, and knowledge are words we often use, but I found it interesting that we don't really know what *knowledge* is. What kind of object is it? What kind of objects is message, information, or meaning?

The Mystery of DNA

It's unanimously accepted that DNA carries instructions for how to construct proteins.

You can appreciate the useful nature of instructions. For example, you read instructions before assembling a piece of new furniture at home to make sure you do it right. Cells do a similar job. They read DNA instructions and then build everything in your body from your internal organs to the hair on top of your head.

Let's say that DNA is the complete set of instructions on how to build a life.

When you read the furniture instructions, you know that the instructions were written by a person with knowledge of how to put together this piece of furniture.

Similar to assembling instructions, genetic code carries knowledge about how to build living beings. Let's think about it. Cells retrieve information (instructions) from the DNA that tells them how to do their job. The interesting question is where does this knowledge come from?

For example, when you read instructions, you create an understanding in your head of how to proceed with the furniture assembly. But your understanding isn't original knowledge. A technical writer possessed that original knowledge and passed it along to you in the form of intelligent instructions.

DNA passes genetic knowledge to cells. Where is this stream of vast genetic life-sustaining knowledge coming from?

According to the science of biology, it's coming out of nowhere.

Archeology vs. Biology

Let's say that archeologists uncover ancient cave drawings of bulls and horses that convey rudimentary knowledge about these animals. What would the archeologists' key hypothesis be about the origin of these drawings? Would they entertain an idea that the random forces of weathering produced these drawings? Or would they believe that it was the work of some intelligent beings, like Neanderthals or early Homo sapiens?

The drawings convey very little information; they just reproduce the shapes of animals. Yet, it would be hard to convince archeologists that the random force of wind and rain could produce figures imbued with such meaning.

DNA holds much more knowledge than any drawing on Earth, including the most technical schematics for space rockets. Would be it so wrong to believe that the vast knowledge of how to build millions of species was produced by some form of intellect?

Archeologists don't believe in the creative capacity of random forces. So why do biologists still believe in it?

5. Jesus' View on the Life's Origin

"The Spirit gives life; the flesh counts for nothing."
(John 6:63)

At first, I didn't understand the meaning of Jesus' words. The statement seemed to be a grandiose but improbable claim. Then I compared it with Newton's laws, and I was shocked. I felt as the sky broke over my head, and I heard the voice of wisdom coming from above.

As Isaac Newton wisely noted, the physical world is a balanced, stable, and predictable place, such that "an object at rest remains at rest unless acted upon by an external force."[vii] The statement is called Newton's first law of motion.

Jesus' conveys a notion that for the phenomenon of life to occur, there must be a proper cause too. He says, *"The Spirit gives life."*

There is a logical resemblance between Jesus' statement and Newton's first law. Both statements communicate a similar meaning: the necessity of a proper cause behind any event in the universe. According to Newton's law, physical motions are caused by physical forces. An object at rest remains at rest unless an external force acts upon it.

Likewise, Jesus insists that the appearance of life can only be caused by an intellectual force. To see the logical similarity between Jesus and Newton's thoughts, let's rephrase Jesus' statement using the style of Newton's law.

> *Physical matter remains non-living (the flesh counts for nothing) unless acted upon by an external creative force (the Spirit gives life).*

According to Jesus, life would never happen of its own accord.

6. Knowledge of the First Kind

Two Kinds of Knowledge

Scientific knowledge comes from observations and thinking. What is religious knowledge?

When Jesus was fasting in the wilderness at the very beginning of his ministry, the devil approached him.

"If you are the Son of God, tell these stones to become bread," the devil said, tempting Jesus.

> Jesus answered, "It is written: 'Man shall not live on bread alone, but on every word that comes from the mouth of God.'" (Matthew 4:4)

Jesus quotes the verse from The Book of Deuteronomy, which separates knowledge into two kinds. The first kind of knowledge is our practical, know-how type of knowledge: How to grow wheat, bake bread, make clothes, and manufacture any type of device. Scientific knowledge fits into this type. We need this kind of knowledge to survive and make our life comfortable.

The second kind of knowledge comes directly from the mouth of God.

The Package Deal

Hypothetically, if God exists, then his knowledge about reality would surpass our own. For this reason, we switch the order: God's knowledge is the first kind, and ours is the second.

Jesus' message about the heavenly kingdom is one among countless other scientific, philosophical, and religious teachings. According to Jesus, his teaching outclasses all others because it carries knowledge of the first kind:

> *Not until halfway through the festival did Jesus go up to the temple courts and begin to teach. The Jews there were amazed and asked, "How did this man get such learning without having been taught?"*
>
> *So Jesus answered them, "My teaching is not mine, but his who sent me." (John 7:14-16 ESV)*

Jesus claimed that he received his knowledge directly from God. It sounds impressive.

Yet, we have two issues here. First, we don't know for certain if God exists. Without believing in God, Jesus' claim makes no sense.

For now we must leave the question of God's existence open.

The second problem is trust. Why should we believe Jesus?

Sometimes people lie. How would we know that Jesus tells truth? Also, maybe Jesus truly believed that he received his teaching from God, but in reality, it was nothing more than a hallucination.

Interestingly enough, Jesus provides evidence supporting his claims:

> *"But if I do his work, believe in the evidence of the miraculous works I have done, even if you don't believe me." (John 10:38 NLT)*

Jesus persuades his listeners to believe in the evidence, even if they don't believe his word. What is the evidence? It's Jesus' ability to perform miracles.

It sounds logical. Jesus' supernatural abilities are the evidence that communication between him and the Heavenly Father did indeed take place. Knowledge of the first kind is a package deal. It comes with heavenly information plus the power of performing miracles. It gives us solid criteria for how to differentiate between a liar and the true God's messenger.

Yet, we're still having the issue here. Maybe Jesus' miracles were enough evidence for the eyewitnesses, but unfortunately, it's not very good evidence for us. The people who saw Jesus' miracles are long since dead. Today, many people doubt that Jesus performed miracles at all. How could you know if the Gospel was telling the truth about Jesus' miraculous works?

Then I thought, "The Gospel of John says that the Jews in the temple were amazed by Jesus' teaching."

If Jesus got his teaching from God, then his preaching should carry knowledge that was far ahead of his time. Can we find such knowledge in the Gospel? Would this knowledge amaze us as it amazed Jews in the temple?

7. The Parable of the Sower

I decided to look into Jesus' parables. I asked myself: is there anything there that reveals a profound truth about reality?

Here is one of Jesus' parables, known as the Parable of the Sower:

> *Then he told them many things in parables, saying: 'A farmer went out to sow his seed.*
>
> *'As he was scattering the seed, some fell along the path, and the birds came and ate it up.*
>
> *'Some fell on rocky places, where it did not have much soil. It sprang up quickly, because the soil was shallow. But when the sun came up, the plants were scorched, and they withered because they had no root.*
>
> *'Other seed fell among thorns, which grew up and choked the plants.*
>
> *'Still other seed fell on good soil, where it produced a crop—a hundred, sixty or thirty times what was sown. Whoever has ears, let them hear.' (Matthew 13:3-9)*

At first, I was taken aback. The parable sounded like a plain old agricultural story. A farmer went out to sow the seed, but he wasn't careful and scattered the seed all over the place. Most of the seed was wasted, since it fell on harsh land that was not suitable for growing crops, and a few fell on good soil. Only the seeds that fell on good soil produced a decent harvest.

It seemed like the parable didn't convey any profound meaning.

The parable was particularly uninspiring because it referenced the hard and routine labor of farmers. Usually, spiritual teachings attract you for the opposite reason. You expect to find an escape from routine tasks.

In addition, the parable uses a sown seed as a metaphor for a message about the heavenly kingdom. The comparison between the message and the seed doesn't seem to be an intuitive metaphor. It's difficult to see a correlation between a message and a seed.

8. Sharing Knowledge

A Message

A message is generally understood as a piece of information communicated to someone. Is the message and information the same thing?

Let's start with a simple example. You look through a window and see a tree. When you think, "I see a tree," you create a new piece of information-knowledge. You're capable of creating a new bit of information by analyzing your observation.

Knowledge is the outcome when observations are understood.

The important feature of information is that it can be shared with other people. To communicate your newly created bits of information, you must craft a message. Let's return to our example; suppose you pick up a phone, call your mother, and say, "I see a tree." You're communicating a message—a piece of information in the stage of transmission.

Duality of Language

When you say, "I see a tree," anyone can easily relate to the observation because we have all seen trees on many occasions.

Jesus' message about the heavenly kingdom is different because you don't have similar observations to draw from. You don't even know what kind of experiences caused Jesus to acquire such information. This is why Jesus' message is outstanding. It communicates information you haven't encountered through your own life experiences. For this same reason, you can't verify his information.

Regardless of how Jesus acquired knowledge about the kingdom of heaven, he chose to communicate it to other people. Language is our preferred tool for communication. Usually, a language is defined as a collection of words and the set of rules for how to put those words together, both in speaking and in writing.

We use language almost as often as we breathe. It seems we should know everything about language. Yet, the most important characteristic of any human language—its dualism—skips entirely our attention.

Besides its theological meaning, the Parable of the Sower also helps us to understand how language works. When explaining the parable, Jesus said,

> *"When anyone hears the message about the kingdom and does not understand it [...]" (Matthew 13:9 NIV)*

Here, Jesus separates hearing and understanding. Hearing is a physical process, in the sense that a spoken word is a sequence of specific sounds that travel through the air. You process these sounds when they reach your ears.

To understand a message, you must know the meaning of the words you've heard. You wouldn't understand the message "Puedo ver un árbol" (I see a tree) if you don't know Spanish.

A word is a dualistic entity because it exists in two forms. First, it exists as a physical sequence of sounds or written letters. But in the second form, our memory associates meaning (information-knowledge) with each word in a language.

When you hear a message, your mind makes sense (new information-knowledge) of the message. This process is called interpretation. You associate each word with its inherent meaning. If a word has a few meanings, you chose the fitting meaning from context. By knowing the meaning of each word and applying rules of grammar, you re-create the meaning of the whole sentence.

Spoken and written words are the physical part of a language, whereas the meanings of words are the intellectual part. Language is dualistic in its nature because it cannot exist without either of these two parts. If no one remembers the meanings of the words, the language dies.

Communication

The task of language is to convey meaning and pass knowledge from the speaker to the listener.

Meaningful communication isn't an easy task. To begin with, you need an observation worthy of sharing. Then you have to craft a message, which cleverly and elegantly conveys the chosen information-knowledge.

During transmission, information is encoded in sounds or symbols. The sound of a voice doesn't carry information; it carries a code. If the message has been heard, it can be converted back into information.

Similarly, the pages of a book don't literally carry information-knowledge. A book is just a bound set of sheets marked with printed letters. When you read the book, your mind re-creates the enclosed knowledge.

To recap, so far, we've established three important facts.

First, knowledge is an intellectual substance. Knowledge only exists inside the mind. No knowledge can be found beyond the mind. For example, books don't preserve knowledge in a literal sense; they preserve a text. When you read a text, you re-create that specific piece of knowledge in your mind.

The second fact is derived from the first: only an intellect can create new knowledge. It should be obvious: if knowledge can exist only inside the mind, then only the mind can create new knowledge.

The third fact is that knowledge can be passed between minds. The process of communication consists of three phases.

- In the first phase, the mind of the speaker (or the writer) creates the initial knowledge and encodes it with the help of language as a message
- In the second phase, information is communicated as speech (or text)
- In the third phase, the mind of the listener (or the reader) decodes the message and re-creates the original information

All three of these facts will help us to understand how genetic code works.

9. The Seed Falling on Good Soil

Life

So what is life and how does information-knowledge relate to it?

The complexity of life is a mystery. For example, non-living structural elements, once abandoned, will decay. Forsaken buildings and cities slowly fall into ruins. At the same time, living beings advance and evolve from simple to complex forms. It's a little bit strange. How could the same forces of nature lead to such conflicting results?

Yes, life conceals a great mystery.

Contemporary biology defines a living creature as something capable of growing, eating, and reproducing. Here a quote from Biology online: "Life is a distinctive characteristic of a living organism from a dead organism or non-living thing, as specifically distinguished by the capacity to grow, metabolize, respond (to stimuli), adapt, and reproduce."[viii]

This definition only describes some of life's features, rather than what life really *is*. Our appreciation of life is often limited to the above—we associate joy in life with eating, drinking, and reproduction.

What did Jesus say about life? Did he reveal any knowledge that was far ahead of his time?

Jesus doesn't fit with our current views and traditions, just as he didn't fit into the customs of his time. Yet, we can hardly call him a rebel. He isn't someone who denies knowledge; he's someone who shows us more. According to Jesus, eating, drinking, and even reproduction aren't essential qualities of life.

In the parable of the Sower, Jesus uses an image of the sown seed to show how the message about the kingdom affects people with a different mindset. Let's look at the parable in reverse order. What does the parable tell us about the sown seed?

> *"But the seed falling on good soil refers to someone who hears the word and understands it." (Matthew 13:23)*

At the beginning of the sentence, Jesus points out that a new life sprouts when a seed falls on good soil. This seems like common knowledge that transcends time and culture. The shocking part is the second half, where Jesus compares life growing from the seed with understanding the message.

Encoded Information

We need to stop for a few moments to observe the similarity between these two events.

Today, we know that life is possible because DNA molecules carry genetic instructions, and cells then use these instructions to build living organisms. It's universally accepted that DNA stores biological information. The genetic code is a set of rules by which DNA information is translated into proteins by living cells.[ix]

We can see that both a message and DNA are similar things; they're encoded streams of information. The types of code are different, and the methods of delivery are different, but in essence, both a message and DNA are the same thing—a piece of code.

Even more, the logical structure of a message and DNA are both similar. A complex message consists of sentences, which are sequences of words that express a complete idea. DNA consists of genes, which are regions of DNA that store information about specific characteristics in an organism. Both techniques of coding split information into smaller logical units.

Isn't it amazing that Jesus compares a growing life to the understanding of the message?

10. Who Made Cells?

This was how I learned that drinking and eating didn't make up the key characteristics of life. Life would never happen if cells couldn't read genetic code.

"Isn't it amazing?" I thought.

In the Parable of the Sower, Jesus uses the image of life growing from a seed. The image highlights the importance of understanding God's message. The one who understands the message and follows it is compared to the seed falling on good soil. As it turns out, the seed produces life because the seed's cells have the ability to understand the encoded DNA message.

The parable helps us understand both how to deal with God's knowledge and also how life works.

I looked in the window and saw a squirrel running across the grass under a tree. Then I saw my neighbor walking his dog in the street.

I can bet that when you see an animal, you might think about anything except the fact that this elegant creature is made up of cells, and those cells can read. Have you ever wondered how cells got their ability to read the genetic code? For example, if nobody teaches a child to speak, a child wouldn't understand the words of language.

So how then did cells get their ability to read, understand, and follow the DNA instructions? Who taught genetic language to the cells?

"Yes, Ben," I thought remembering my friend and imagining our debate, "who taught genetic language to cells?"

But what good is asking Ben? He is useless. He can't answer this question. I wanted to face the main evolutionary biologist of the country and ask her or him this question. Who taught genetic language to cells?

Children learn letters in school. They learn how to put letters together and make a word. This is how they acquire the skill to read.

Computers know how to read computer code and how to execute it. They know it because both computers and computer code were made this way by computer scientists and software developers.

Cells know how to read genetic code and how to execute it, but how did it happen? Who made them in this amazing way? I wanted to ask it the main evolutionary biologist of the world.

A code is a system of communication in which arbitrarily chosen words, letters, or symbols are assigned definite meanings.

The genetic code is a system of communication that transfers genetic information to living cells. The genetic code consists of three-letter combinations of nucleotides called codons; each codon is a symbol that is infused with meaning—it corresponds to a specific amino acid (or stop signal). Cells are capable of associating a symbol (a three-letter combination of nucleotides) with its meaning (a specific amino acid or stop signal).

But the question remained: who made cells in this way that they know the meaning of codons?

11. The Missing Phase

The Three Phases of Communication

The ability of cells to decode is a problem on its own merits. Yet, DNA presents an even bigger issue.

As we've discovered in previous chapters, communication consists of three phases. In the first phase, the initial knowledge is created and encoded. In the second phase, information is communicated as a written or verbal message. In the third phase, the message is decoded, and our minds re-create the original information.

Now let's look at the genetic code.

DNA conveys information by means of code, which fits nicely into the second phase.

The various cells of your body read these encoded instructions and take action (i.e., build more liver cells or repair the cut on our thumb). This reading and re-creating information is clearly the third phase.

The problem is we're missing the first phase—the phase when genetic information was created and encoded.

Evolutionary biology proposes a sensational idea that you don't need this first phase. Random changes don't need to know the meaning of the DNA message. They can construct the meaningfully encoded message without knowing its meaning and without knowing the rules of encoding.

It's a rather radical proposition.

All human languages are nothing but a specific type of code. If you read an article that conveys expert knowledge on any subject, you'd never doubt that it was written by an intelligent writer. But what if an article was written with a different type of code, let's say, a genetic code?

Just think about it: DNA delivers expert knowledge on the subject of life to cells.

Now let me ask you these questions, should this expert knowledge have some kind of origin? What could this origin be?

The Second Rule

According to Newton's second rule of reasoning, "The same natural effects we must, as far as possible, assign to the same causes."[x]

Let's return to our earlier example and imagine that you are holding some furniture instructions. Somewhere in an overseas factory, a technical writer learned how this specific piece of furniture should be assembled and then wrote the instructions.

The little booklet is the effect. The capacity of the writer to record his understandings in the form of instructions is the cause.

Now, DNA is also an effect. What's more important, DNA does a similar job as the furniture manual; it delivers encoded instructions. Isaac Newton recommends that we assign similar causes to similar effects.

I don't know what it tells you, but it tells me that Isaac Newton would never choose random mutations as the possible cause of DNA. He would prefer to believe in the Intelligent Writer.

12. In the Beginning

Logos

"In the beginning was the Word, and the Word was with God, and the Word was God." (John 1:1)

The English term "word" is used here to translate the Greek word *logos* (λόγος).

The word "logos" has dual meanings. It refers either to thoughts, which are put together in the mind or to the same thoughts expressed as words.[xi] When it refers to the thought, the word "logos" corresponds to the state of mind when a logical structure of a situation is clearly understood.

When the apostle John said, "In the beginning was the Logos," he most likely was referring to the original creative thought (or as we would say in this book, information-knowledge). He intended to point to the beginning of things, and he knew that a thought precedes a spoken word (a message). The English translation is slightly misleading because the term "word" is used only in the meaning of vocal or written expressions.

It would be more accurate to say, "In the beginning was the thought (the collection of ideas, information-knowledge, understanding)."

John continues,

"Through him all things were made; without him nothing was made that has been made." (John 1:3 NIV)

John proclaims that new things cannot be made without preceding knowledge. "Through him (Logos, the entity holding the knowledge) all things were made; without him, nothing was made that has been made."

The Source of Knowledge

Nothing meaningful can be made without prior thinking.

It's true that a toddler can push keyboard buttons. But why can't she produce a functional computer code? Because she lacks the necessary knowledge, which an experienced software developer has. The ability to randomly push keyboard buttons isn't enough to develop an application code.

The ability to randomly push keyboard buttons isn't enough to write a set of furniture instructions.

I hope all evolutionary biologists would agree that the ability to randomly push keyboard buttons isn't enough to write a scientific article.

To produce a meaningful message, you must first come up with the meaning.

The apostle John voiced the exact same idea (only two thousand years earlier—isn't it amazing?): *"In the beginning was the Logos."* In the beginning was knowledge. In the beginning of the universe was knowledge. In the beginning of life was knowledge.

The recent scientific discovery of DNA can be viewed as spectacular evidence supporting John's thesis. DNA delivers expert knowledge on the subject of life to cells. According to John, knowledge preceded the creation of genetic code. And knowledge was with God.

Maybe you shouldn't disregard the wisdom of the ancient saints. Maybe you need to accept John's statements as containing two key cognitive principles. First, knowledge always precedes any type of message or meaningful code. Second, intellect and nothing else creates new knowledge, even in the case when DNA delivers it.

13. Made in Heaven

The Fossil Record

Once I cleaned and organized my notes, I wrote an email to Ben.

"I am pleased to inform you that the theory of evolution is incorrect. The genetic code passes information between generations. Yet, to create the first original DNA without knowing information that needed to be encoded is impossible. You also must understand the rules of coding. All this tells you that life was created by an intellect. For details, please see the attached file."

I attached my file and sent the email.

A few days later, Ben replied.

"Don't be silly. Evolution is a fact. Check the fossil record."

"He didn't read the file," I thought and began typing a reply.

"Yes, the fossil record shows that changes have been happening. But we don't know *how* these changes were inflicted. It's more likely that the DNA of new species was developed by an unknown supreme intellect rather than by random…"

I stopped typing. What am I doing? Ben wasn't interested in any proof.

I deleted the text and typed: "I've checked the fossil record, and it was stamped 'Made in heaven.'"

Ben replied next day, "You've checked the wrong record. Get out of the church's basement, find a museum of natural history, and check it there."

I laughed. I felt great.

I began my inquiry into the theory of evolution with the hope that I would find contradictions, which I needed to overcome my own doubts. Strangely enough, I had found the flow. The theory of evolution is solely based on the logical fallacy that random changes could generate meaningful code.

It was night. I was sitting at the kitchen in front of my laptop.

"So, what now?" I thought.

I switched the light off, went to the window, and looked at a sleepy street with rows of big old trees on both sides. I saw a few dim lights in the windows of the houses standing behind the trees. My neighbors were still living in the routine world, but I knew that routine was an illusion.

"Reality isn't limited to this," I said, looking at the street.

I felt wonderful. Reality turned out to be much deeper than I used to believe, and I had proof in my notes.

The Power of Knowledge

For the next few weeks, ideas kept coming into my head.

It was a great period in my spiritual-intellectual development. Jesus' sayings and parables were like pieces of an intricate jigsaw puzzle, and suddenly, they started coming together.

For example, Jesus says,

"My teaching is not my own. It comes from the one who sent me." (John 7:16)

"Alright," I thought, "Jesus insists that he got his teaching from the Heavenly Father."

According to our terminology, Jesus' teachings is knowledge of the first kind.

In the parable of the Sower, Jesus compares his teaching with the sown seed. Today, you know about DNA and genetic code. You might notice an additional layer of meaning.

DNA delivers biological know-how to cells in the form of a complete set of instructions. Let's say that the Absolute Mind of God created this knowledge. On the other hand, Jesus got his teaching from the Heavenly Father also. It means that both Jesus' teaching and DNA deliver knowledge of the first kind.

Astonishing, isn't it? Now, we can see why Jesus compares his teaching with the seed.

Furthermore, the parable tells us another fascinating thing: Knowledge of the first kind produces life.

When cells read DNA instructions, the encoded knowledge produces biological life.

When a human soul lives "*on every word that comes from the mouth of God,*" God's knowledge presumably produces eternal spiritual life.

14. Jesus' Take on Motivation

God-to-Human Communication

The Parable of the Sower deals with a God-to-human type of communication.

It should be similar to a human-to-human type of communication because the transfer of knowledge happens between two minds. However, we suspect that the qualities of intellect differ from supreme on God's end to mediocre (or worse) on our end.

What stands out here is the methodology of God's communication. The Heavenly Father chose only one individual to entrust his knowledge to, and then the chosen one communicated God's message to the rest of us.

Jesus' preaching is a usual human-to-human type of communication. Let's call it communication of the second kind. The initial God-to-human communication supposedly happened between the Heavenly Father and Jesus. This would be the communication of the first kind.

The technical details of this type of communication are a mystery to us. Did it happen through language, and if so, was it a human language or God's language? How would Jesus know God's language? How would God know human language? How was the voice of God transmitted?

We don't know. Technical questions aren't our biggest concern. They usually can be solved if there is a conceptual solution to the problem. For example, if the Heavenly Father exists, then He finds a way to communicate his message.

The importance of understanding God's message and following it is the main theme of the Parable of the Sower.

Role of Motivation

To move a physical object, one needs to apply an external force. People have known this at an intuitive level since the dawn of time. When Newton formulated the first law of motion, he created a logical understanding—or, as the ancient Greeks would say, logos.

Another intuitively well-known fact is that a strong enough reason can move people's souls. Most of the messages you encounter daily are designed to motivate you.

Politicians motivate citizens to trust them. Advertisements motivate customers to buy products. Business leaders motivate their employees to be loyal and productive. Romantic partners motivate each other to stay faithful and committed.

These motivational messages try to convince you to take some action—to vote, to buy, to work harder. Other people want you to do something for their benefit. A motivational component is perceived as the main function of the church. A pastor motivates the parish on Sunday to be good during the next week.

Jesus

Jesus stands apart from others in his take on motivational strategies.

Imagine that you came in the midday heat, from a town a few miles away, to see Jesus. You've heard plenty of rumors about him, so now you want to see the miracles he does. By the time you get there, "such a large crowd gathered around him that he got into a boat and sat in it, while all the people stood on the shore" (Matthew 13:2 NIV).

While you stand in the crowd, he tells the Parable of the Sower. The parable is literally saying that only a seed falling on good soil produces a good crop. Living in an agricultural region, you would already know that. You might be disappointed.

The situation could be seen as comical because of the complete failure of the disciples to grasp Jesus' attitude. The large crowds gathered to hear the teaching of God's messenger. They'd been standing there since early morning. They were tired and hungry but full of religious excitement. They were eager to see miracles, to be inspired by unusual signs, to be emotionally moved by the power of God.

Then Jesus got out of the house, walked to the lake, jumped in a boat, and told them the story about the sower with bad aim.

Instead of motivating his listeners to worship God, Jesus told them the parable that (seemingly) lacks any motivational strength.

Jesus' disciples became concerned. They came to him and asked,

"Why do you speak to the people in parables?" (Matthew 13:10)

Instead of using this opportunity to recruit more followers, Jesus bored his listeners with an irrelevant story. What was he expecting the crowds to do? Turn away and go home with disappointment in their hearts?

Obviously, Jesus understood the role of motivation. His mission was to bring people to God, not turn them away. Then what was the matter?

You seek to motivate other people when you want them to do something beneficial for you like working harder or buying your product. Jesus displays an indifferent attitude towards the crowd's desire to see miracles. He lets everyone know that he isn't a motivational speaker. He has no plans to motivate anybody.

Sometimes you might think that God needs you and your attention. But the wellbeing of the heavenly kingdom doesn't depend on your favors. The kingdom doesn't seek to motivate anybody. The kingdom doesn't need you. The order of things is reversed. You're in need and, therefore, you should seek the kingdom. You should seek how to motivate the kingdom of heaven to become interested in your persona.

You need to inspire the kingdom's interest in your soul.

Soon I found out that spiritual self-motivation wasn't an easy task. You don't miss the things you don't know. For example, you know from experience that traveling is a lot of fun. For this reason, you travel on your vacations.

On the contrary, you have no practical knowledge about the kingdom of heaven and eternal life. The lack of information puts you in a difficult situation. You need to readjust your life and sacrifice many pleasant things for the sake of the heavenly kingdom you know nothing about. How should you go about motivating yourself?

Appendixes

1. The Spiritual Method of Inquiry

Finally, I found Jesus' take on the spiritual method of inquiry,

> *"Ask, and it will be given to you; seek, and you will find; knock, and it will be opened to you." (Matthew 7:7 ESV)*

It begins, similarly to the scientific method, with questioning. The difference is that science studies external physical objects, whereas Jesus recommends asking inner spiritual questions.

In the beginning of my inquiry, I asked if it fits a reasonable person to believe in God. I found the answer: only an intellectual input could create and improve DNA. The stream of genetic knowledge should come from some intelligent source, right?

Also, I wanted to find firm evidence of God because I knew that educated people should believe in theories that are supported by evidence. Slowly, I realized that evidence wasn't a sure thing either. For example, is the fact that DNA delivers genetic information to cells strong enough evidence to you that life is a product of knowledge?

Evidence must be understood, analyzed, and interpreted by somebody. Interpretation is a tricky thing because your reading of evidence depends on your current system of beliefs. I believe that DNA can't appear without prior knowledge. You have a different mindset and you might come up with different explanations of the same fact.

You find what you seek.

Testing

Similar to the scientific method, the religious method involves testing. The difference is that external objects and forces are subjects to scientific testing, whereas you are the subject of the spiritual tests, which are also known under name of temptation.

Many years have peacefully passed by and suddenly, testing of my beliefs came in the form of the MRNA vaccine mandate.

"God created human DNA," I thought. "Any unauthorized unnatural modification of the latter violates His intellectual rights. Protection of your DNA is your God-given right and your responsibility."

It costed me my previous job and moving to another country in search for employment but, hey, what can you do? You don't want to fail your spiritual inquiry at the phase of testing, right?

2. The Root of the Tree of Life

In philosophy, dualism is the position that explains phenomena by two opposing principles.[xii] For example, to explain the mind-body problem, dualists say that the mind is a group of functions that correlate to the brain. However, the mind cannot be reduced to the physical elements and is therefore a distinct non-physical entity.[xiii]

Physicalists, however, say that the mind will eventually be explained in terms of physical matter and energies.[xiv]

Duality of Light

"While you have the light, believe in the light, that you may become sons of light." (John 12:36 ESV)

Jesus uses light as a metaphor for spirit and intellect. Light symbolizes the capacity to think clearly. Understanding is the mental equivalent of physical vision.

Sometimes you say "I see" in the meaning "I understand." Light helps you to see. Intellect is the light within that enables you to understand the invisible circumstances of your situation.

Without light, the universe would be a horrible place, and without the capacity to understand, you wouldn't be called a human.

Interestingly enough, light displays a dualistic nature. In physics, it's called the wave/particle duality of light. According to scientific observations, every elementary particle exhibits the properties of both particles and waves. In this scientific view, it's understood that light travels away from a source as an electromagnetic wave, but the moment it impacts an object, the entire wave disappears, and a photon particle appears.[xv]

That being said, the duality of light isn't an exact case of dualism, because both an electromagnetic field and a photon are physical elements.

Dualism of Language

It gets even more interesting.

Jesus uses light as a symbol of intellect. The key function of intellect is to create knowledge. Knowledge is communicated by means of human language. Language is an example of *actual* dualism because a word has two entirely different forms: physical and intellectual.

When you speak, the sound of your voice travels away from your mouth as an acoustic (physical) wave. When your listeners understand the meaning of the words they hear, their minds create bits of knowledge. The sequence of letters or sounds is the physical form of the word, and meaning is the intellectual form.

It brings us to an amazing coincidence: Both physical light and the light of knowledge exhibit duality when transmitted.

And that's not all.

It's universally accepted that DNA stores biological information. We might have different opinions on the origin of this information, but DNA offers another example of dualism.

In this case, biological information that cells retrieve from DNA is the intellectual element, whereas the molecular structure of DNA that conveys this information is the physical element. Similar to human languages, DNA displays duality.

The tree of life is rooted in information and knowledge. Isn't it fascinating?

~ If you like this book, please leave a review ~

Acknowledgements

I would like to express my gratitude to everyone who provided support in writing this book; everyone who read, proofread, and offered comments and edits.

Above all, I want to thank my wife for her patience, love, and support.

If you would like to support this independent author, please buy his other equally thoughtful and entertaining books:

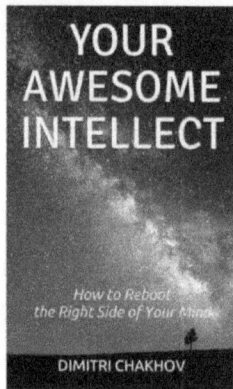

Your Awesome Intellect: *How to Reboot the Right Side of Your Mind*

YOUR AWESOME INTELLECT

How to Reboot the Right Side of Your Mind

DIMITRI CHAKHOV

Modern philosophers often see the human inner-self—or consciousness—as an illusion.

In this book, the author seeks a meaningful vision of life. He believes that his mind is real. Unexpectedly, he finds support for his thoughts in the Gospels.

In a nutshell, Jesus rejects a materialistic worldview. He teaches that the creativity of your intellect is a sensational force. Your intellectual talent enables you to think and to grow spiritually. Jesus promises that an ingenious and evolving soul will be invited to enter into a different state of being—the *eternal* state...

Being a skeptic, the author asks, "How does Jesus prove his spectacular teaching?"

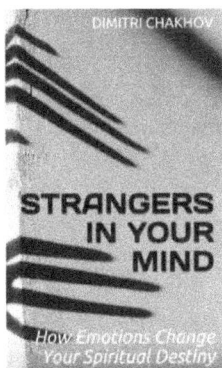

Strangers in Your Mind: *How Emotions Change Your Spiritual Destiny*

Why can't you always keep your cool? It is so easy for your emotions to get out of control. One episode of jealousy or fear could ruin your reputation for a long time.

In this book, the author observes his own emotions. Sometimes he feels that his emotions are trying to dupe him. But why would his own feelings deceive him? The author, who is a computer programmer and scientific-minded skeptic, finds a surprising answer in an ancient religious book.

It turns out that negative emotions aren't just annoying nonsense that wrecks your image. There is a much stronger reason to avoid them at all costs...

Notes

[i] THAYER'S GREEK LEXICON, Electronic Database. (2011) by Biblesoft, Inc. Also available at http://biblehub.com/thayers/4151.htm

[ii] Martin Luther, Table Talk

[iii] Davies, Paul (2005). The mind of God: the scientific basis for a rational world (1st Simon & Schuster pbk. ed.). New York: Simon & Schuster. ISBN 0-671-79718-2.

[iv] TechTarget, (accessed at August 1, 2016), http://searchsoftwarequality.techtarget.com/definition/garbage-in-garbage-out

[v] Dictionary.com Unabridged. Based on the Random House Dictionary, © Random House, Inc. 2016. Also available at www.dictionary.com

[vi] Collins English Dictionary – Complete and Unabridged, 12th Edition (2014) © HarperCollins Publishers. Also available at http://www.collinsdictionary.com/dictionary/english

[vii] Isaac Newton, The Principia (Mathematical Principles of Natural Philosophy), 1687

[viii] Biology-Online, Biology-Online.org (accessed July 27, 2016) http://www.biology-online.org/dictionary/Life

[ix] Purcell, Adam. "DNA". Basic Biology

[x] Isaac Newton, Principia: Rules of Reasoning in Natural Philosophy, Trans. A. Motte, 1729

[xi] THAYER'S GREEK LEXICON, Electronic Database. (2011) by Biblesoft, Inc. Also available at http://biblehub.com/thayers/3056.htm

[xii] Dictionary.com Unabridged. Based on the Random House Dictionary, © Random House, Inc. 2016.

[xiii] Hart, W.D. (1996) "Dualism", in A Companion to the Philosophy of Mind, ed. Samuel Guttenplan, Oxford: Blackwell, pp. 265-7.

[xiv] Daniel Stoljar, "Physicalism", plato.standford.edu (accessed August 1, 2016) http://plato.stanford.edu/entries/physicalism/

[xv] Wikipedia, The Free Encyclopedia, s.v. "Wave-particle duality," (accessed August 1, 2016), https://en.wikipedia.org/wiki/Wave%E2%80%93particle_duality

www.ingramcontent.com/pod-product-compliance
Lightning Source LLC
Chambersburg PA
CBHW021145020426
42331CB00005B/898